Handmade
Embossed
Greetings Cards
Using Stencils

This book is dedicated with love to my
wonderful Mum Jill Baylis, who has always
encouraged and supported my ideas, even
when they were as zany as penguins!

Also in loving memory of my gran, Louise
Carwardine, and my aunt Pat Butler.

Handmade
Embossed
Greetings Cards
Using Stencils

Carol Wallis

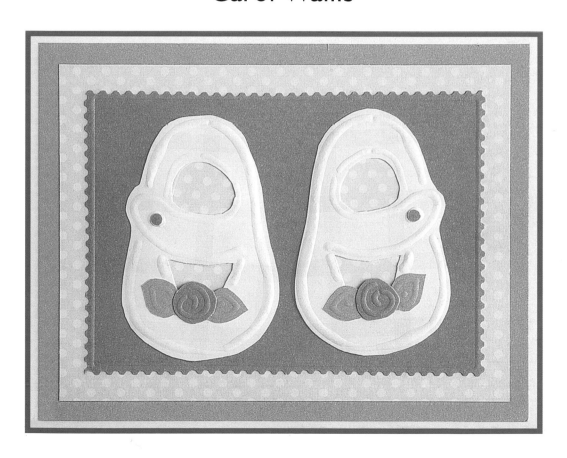

SEARCH PRESS

First published in Great Britain 2004

Search Press Limited
Wellwood, North Farm Road,
Tunbridge Wells, Kent TN2 3DR

Text copyright © Carol Wallis 2004

Photographs by Jon Firth, Search Press Studios and
Roddy Paine Photographic Studios

Photographs and design copyright © Search Press Ltd. 2004

ISBN 1 903975 74 3

The Publishers and author can accept no responsibility for any
consequences arising from the information, advice or
instructions given in this publication.

Suppliers
If you have difficulty in obtaining any of the materials and
equipment mentioned in this book, then please visit the
Search Press website for details of suppliers:
www.searchpress.com

Alternatively, you can write to the Publishers at the address
above, for a current list of stockists, including firms who
operate a mail-order service.

Publishers' note
All the step-by-step photographs in this book feature the
author, Carol Wallis, demonstrating how to make
embossed greetings cards. No models have been used.

Printed in Spain by A. G. Elkar S. Coop. 48180 Loiu (Bizkaia)

*I would like to thank Maggie Wright, who asked me
to do my first demonstration and started me on a
new career; Julie Hickey and Melanie Hendrick who
first mentioned me to Search Press; Linda and
Nigel Guest of The Craft Barn who support my
creativity and allow me to enjoy the thrill of teaching
in their studio; Gromit and Mo for always being
there and for caring; Mandy, Nikki and Fifi for going
along with my mad ideas; Sue Taylor and Mel Peters
for being brilliant sisters; Lynell Harlow of
Dreamweaver Stencils and Peter Clark at Kars & Co
for their generosity; Judith Brewer at Woodware for
providing me with products; Lasting Impressions for
allowing me to use their stencils, and all my crafting
friends who are too numerous to list individually.*

*I also want to thank the team at Search Press,
particularly commissioning editor Roz Dace for
having faith in me and Juan, Rachel and Jon for
their hard work during photography. I especially
want to thank my editor Alison Howard for her
patience and help. Without the support and
encouragement I received from everyone this book
would never have become a reality. Thank you.*

Cover

3D Daisy

*This variation of the Daisy, Daisy project (see page 12) was
mounted using 3D foam tape to give a relief effect.*

Page 1

Hot Metal

*This variation of the Hot Metal project (see page 24) was
worked on card for a completely different effect.*

Page 3

Tiny Toes

*This card decorated with a little pair of rosebud-trimmed
shoes can be made by following the instructions on page 36.*

Page 5

Daisy Swirls

*The complementary colours green and purple used for this
variation of the Daisy, Daisy project (see page 12), really
make it 'zing'.*

Contents

Introduction

For everyone who has nagged me for the last few years to write a book: this is for you!

I started crafting several years ago but, after dabbling in many different crafts, I found myself looking for something new. Luckily, I was visiting my local craft store when a very brief demonstration of stencil embossing was given. Short though it was – only over a lunch break – it was enough for me to be hooked! I bought some brass stencils and an embossing tool, and began a passion that has been with me ever since.

At first I had no books, instructions or tutor so I taught myself. Though I made lots of mistakes, somehow good things always emerged from them, so it was a relatively painless process. Almost before I knew it, I was producing professional cards that were inspiring others to want to learn stencil embossing, which is also known as dry embossing.

I have not looked back since the owner of my local craft store asked *me* to give an in-store demonstration. From little acorns, as the saying goes, and before long I began to teach and demonstrate regularly. I have made live television appearances and written articles for magazines, and I also demonstrate regularly at craft shows. I love the challenge of thinking up different ways to use stencils, and I really enjoy meeting all the people who are curious enough to come and see what I do.

One of the best things about this craft is that anyone can do it. My youngest student so far was five, and the oldest eighty-four! Both of them produced fantastic cards in next to no time. It gives me a real thrill when other people discover how simple it is to create beautiful cards, and to see their pride in what they have achieved.

I hope you enjoy making the projects in this book as much as I did, and that they will inspire you to create lots of beautiful cards.

Carol

These cards for all occasions are simple, fast and fun to make using the methods shown in this book.

Materials

There is a huge choice of stencils suitable for embossing. Most are made of brass or coated brass like those used for the projects, but plastic stencils are also available. Brass stencils are comparatively expensive, but if you look after them they should last a lifetime. Keep the packaging and replace your stencil in it after use to keep it in pristine condition. Some stencils have only one motif, while others incorporate several. If you choose stencils that complement each other you will be able to mix elements of two or more designs. For this type of stencil you will need a light box for embossing.

Light boxes come in many different types, sizes and styles, and are illuminated either by fluorescent tubes or low-wattage bulbs. They are not just for photographers – I would be lost without mine. Before I bought it, my light source was the window. It made my arms ache and restricted my embossing activities to the daytime! You can also use a glass-topped table lit from below and covered with grease-proof paper to protect your eyes from the glare and the table from scratches.

There are also embossing systems that can be used without a light box. These comprise templates that are pushed together to produce a raised image, but have not been used in this book.

Note

Some brands of stencil are fixed to the backing card used to package them with very sticky tape, and can be difficult to remove without bending. The best way is to hold the stencil firmly between thumb and forefinger at the point where the tape is, then peel the backing card away from the stencil rather than the other way round.

Card

I have a huge collection of paper, card and vellum and can never resist any opportunity to add to it. Most of my designs are worked on just a quarter of a sheet, with the card mount made from a folded half-sheet.

Card is usually sold in A4 sheets. Some brands are slightly smaller but you should still be able to make four cards from one piece as the stencils are not very large.

A wide range of stencils is available, and with care these can be mixed and matched to add interest to your work.

Embellishments

I use lots of extra bits and pieces to decorate my cards, including narrow ribbon, thread, tiny buttons, gems, beads, wire and even tiny 'wobbly eyes'. You may have these items in your workbox.

Eyelets are a useful way to join card instead of glue and are especially good for vellum, which may be marked by adhesive. Bradlets fasten in a similar way but are often more decorative. See page 34–35 for variations using eyelets and bradlets.

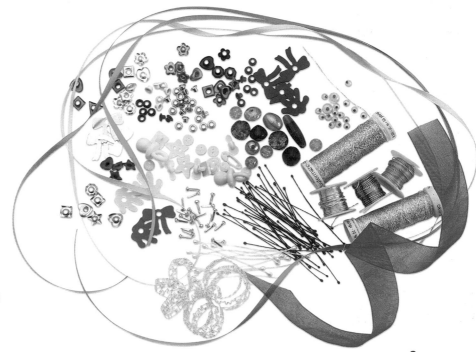

Equipment

Light box These are available in various sizes. I use a small battery operated light box which has the advantage of being easily portable.

Use **corner rounders** to produce perfect, neat rounded corners and **hole punches** to make neat holes to thread ribbon or wire through, or to punch out tiny dots for use in projects.

Scissors should feel comfortable in the hand. You will need different sizes. **Fancy craft scissors** add a decorative touch to edges.

I use **tacky craft adhesive** to stick card and paper and **PVA adhesive** to fill large areas (see page 26). **Spray adhesive** is useful for layering work, especially on vellum. There are two types of **glitter adhesive**: 'dries white' helps to keep the colour of glitter true when used on dark card and 'dries clear' is best for light or white card. '**Glitter glue**' is ultra-fine glitter mixed with adhesive in a nozzle bottle.

Adhesive tape is available on rolls or useful dispensers. Use **double-sided tape** to join layers of card and paper and **low-tack 'removable' tape** to fix stencils without damaging the card. **Double-sided foam tape** can be used to give work a 3D effect. Special **vellum tape** can be used to stick vellum invisibly to card or paper.

Pastel chalks add soft, subtle colour to your raised images, or use ordinary eye-shadows. **Pigment inks** usually come in pads. Apply them sparingly with a tiny brush, and clean the brush with a drop of neat dish-washing liquid. **Felt-tipped pens** are an easy way to add colour. Use **chisel-tipped metallic pens** for the edges of cards, or take the colour off with a fine brush and apply it to your work. Add detail like animals' eyes or the veins on petals with **ultra-fine tipped colour pens.**

Keep a selection of **brushes and applicators**, including large soft brushes to brush off chalk or glitter, tiny **stencilling brushes** to apply pigment ink and **fine brushes** for detail work. **Cotton balls** are useful for blending chalk or applying it to large areas. **Sponge applicators** made for eye-shadow are ideal for applying chalk, and far cheaper than those sold in specialist craft shops. **Cotton buds** (not shown) are also suitable.

A **small guillotine** saves time when trimming card and paper, or use a **metal ruler** and a **craft knife** with a **self-healing cutting mat.**

Hammers and setting tools are used to fix eyelets to your work. **Embossing tools** come in various sizes and types. For working on card they are usually double-ended with metal ball tips: unless otherwise stated the larger ball is the one you will use. Wooden or plastic tools are best used with metal foils: mark the outline with a **cocktail stick** before embossing, and work on the reverse of a **mouse mat** when embossing metal.

Embossing ink is a clear, sticky fluid in a pad. It is dabbed over metal surfaces to adhere the **embossing powder**, which comes in a wide range of colours. 'Cook' the ink and powder with a **heat gun** until it melts. This looks like a hairdryer, and blows out intense heat very gently.

Miscellaneous

Use a **wooden clothes peg** to save burning your fingers when heating metal sheets. A **bone folder** will help you to crease card or paper neatly. Angled **tweezers** are good for removing backing from tape and for placing small decorations or pieces of foam tape. You can use a **pencil** to mark out fold lines on the back of your card, but do not mark the front as the lines are hard to remove. When embossing vellum, a **white crayon** used on the reverse will make the lines look whiter. A **chalk eraser** is useful for removing stray marks and **adhesive putty** will whisk away traces of chalk dust or stray brush hairs. Rub the back of your stencil first with **wax paper** (not shown) to help the embossing tool glide more smoothly, or use a plain white candle.

Daisy, Daisy

This is a good design to start with as it uses only one sheet of card and one stencil. The stencil is moved around so that its different elements form a pleasing composition. Colour is added using chalk, starting with the lightest and building up to the darkest. Use a chalk eraser to remove any stray marks before assembling the finished card. To give a professional-looking finish and a raised effect, the completed design is mounted on layers of card, each of which is edged with a different colour.

If you are worried about mounting the layers evenly, a good tip is to place the top left corner of each card first, which makes it easier to line up. This is because, if you read from left to right, your eye is automatically drawn to that area.

The chalks

The stencil I used

You will need

Daisy stencil: Lasting Impressions L528

White card about 19 x 15 cm (7½ x 6in) for mount

White card, two pieces each about 15 x 8cm (6 x 3¾in)

Low-tack adhesive tape

Wax paper sheet

Light box

Embossing tool with large ball tip

Sponge-tipped applicators

Chalk: light, medium and deep yellow; orange; light and medium green

Craft knife or scalpel and cutting mat, and / or small craft guillotine

Cotton ball

Adhesive putty

Double-sided adhesive tape

Chalk eraser

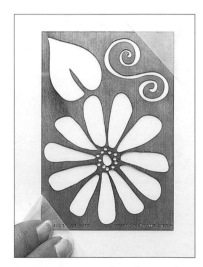

1. Fix the stencil to the card with low-tack adhesive tape.

2. Flip the card and place it on the light box. Apply wax to the back of the design.

3. Using the large ball of the embossing tool, work round the long sides and the top of the stencil. Emboss the flower and swirl, but not the leaf.

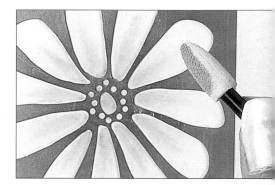

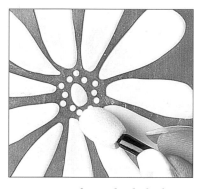

4. Remove from the light box and flip, leaving the stencil in place. Stroke pale yellow chalk on the flower centre and part-way down the petals.

5. Add mid-yellow chalk, but do not take it so far down each petal. Work from the base of the petal towards the tip.

6. Add deep yellow chalk, using just a little towards the centre of each petal.

7. Holding the applicator upright, dab orange chalk in the flower centre and stroke a faint line down each petal.

8. Colour the swirl in blended greens. Remove the stencil.

9. Reposition the stencil so the leaf is at the bottom of the card.

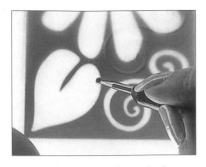

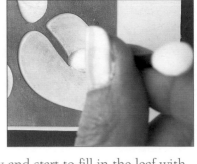

10. Flip your work and place on the light box. Apply wax over the leaf and emboss it.

11. Take the card off the light box and start to fill in the leaf with light green. Add dark green from the centre outwards but not right to the edge.

12. Reposition the stencil so the second swirl mirrors the first. Place on the light box, wax and emboss. Remove from the light box and colour in the second swirl.

13. Replace the stencil in its original position. Working on the light box, wax and emboss the remaining outline at the lower edge of the card, but do not go over the leaf shape.

14. Use adhesive putty to remove any tape residue from your work.

15. Replace the stencil and, using a cotton ball, rub on a blend of yellow chalks to colour the edge. Do not tape the stencil down for this stage.

16. Edge the second small piece of card with green chalk, then fold the mount card in half and colour the front edges with deep yellow chalk.

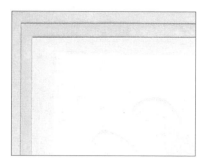

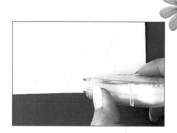

17. Trim 6mm (¼in) from the edge of the project card using a craft knife or guillotine. Trim 3mm (⅛in) from the card with the green edge.

18. Layer the cards on the card mount to check the effect. Fix the cards in place, a layer at a time, using double-sided tape.

Note
You can buy double-sided tape in a small dispenser, which is a useful and economical way to attach designs to a card mount.

The finished card

Card and matching envelope

The matching envelope was produced very simply by colouring the edges of a plain white envelope with yellow chalk, then laying on the stencil and chalking in the leaves. When you do this, use a spare piece of card to prevent the flap being marked by the chalk.

It is really easy to change the look of this card by using different colours of chalk for the design, or by using metallic or pearlised card. Remove any stray chalk marks or dust afterwards using a chalk eraser. There is no need to fix the chalk.

These examples show how you can move the stencils around to create different designs, and how changing the colours of the chalk can give a completely different effect. The purple daisy card (below left and cover) has been given a 3D effect using the techniques covered in the Tiny Toes project (see page 36), with a simple torn paper base. The delicate blue card in the centre was produced on vellum using the techniques covered in the Icing on the Cake project (see page 30).

Cool Cat

Many stencils are made as a rectangle with the shape inside, and the outside edge can also be used as a template for a frame. Other stencils are simply made in the shape of the animal, flower, bird or whatever. A lot of people are daunted by frameless stencils, and do not understand how to use them. This project shows you all you need to know, and the result is a shaped card that will stand up.

When you place the stencil on the card, make sure you leave a good space between it and the edge of the card. When you cut out the card after colouring it, you must leave a good border to make the embossed line stand out. If you do not, the embossed effect will be lost.

This cat stencil is one of my favourites, and I have used it over and over again. Change the colour of the card or coloured chalk to make your cat as fanciful as you like, or make a card that looks like a favourite moggy. The choice is yours!

You will need

Cat stencil: Kars EK1504

Rectangle of cream card
24 x 18cm (9½ x 7in)

Low-tack adhesive tape

Wax paper sheet

Light box

Embossing tool with large
ball tip

Felt-tipped permanent marker
pens: black, pink and green

Gold felt-tipped pen for bell

Chalk: mid-yellow and two
shades of brown

Sponge-tipped applicators

Ruler

Scissors

Fine brush

Cotton ball

PVA adhesive

The chalks

Note

When you add the chalk to the
outline of the cat, stroke it all on
in the same direction.

The stencil I used

18

1. Fix the stencil to the right front of a card using removable low-tack adhesive tape.

2. Flip the stencil and card over and place on a light box to reveal the design.

3. Rub the back of the card gently with the wax paper sheet.

4. Go round the outline with the embossing tool, then go over the body details.

5. Take the card off the light box and flip it. Fill in the eyes and body details using black pen.

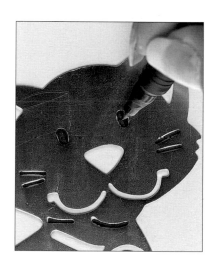

6. Fill in the features using pink pen and the collar using green. Using a fine brush, take some gold ink from the tip of the pen and apply to the bell.

7. Allow to dry, then lift the stencil carefully off the card. The highlight on the nose is made by leaving a tiny area of paper not coloured.

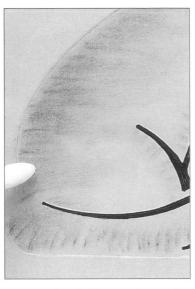

8. Score the card using a ruler and the point of a pair of scissors, then fold so the back of the cat is right on the fold.

9. Using a sponge applicator, stroke on light yellow chalk just inside the embossed line and round the cat's legs.

10. Apply chalk at right angles to the edge of the stencil to produce stripes. Use as many colours as you like and always start with the lightest shade.

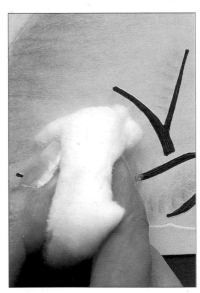

11. As you apply each new colour for the stripes, use a cotton ball to blend it and soften the effect, working with a sweeping stroke.

12. Leaving the card folded, cut carefully round the design but not the strip by the base of the tail. Cut through both layers, leaving a good margin outside the embossed line.

13. Use a craft knife and cutting mat to give a sharp effect round the whiskers. Add a few tiny dots using a fine-tipped black felt pen.

The finished card

Tiny cards and gift tags

A beautiful tag or tiny card can make all the difference to a small gift. The cards have been decorated with different embellishments, including wobbly eyes and raised glitter. Make a tag to coordinate with a card by using a smaller stencil with a similar theme. Or take one element of a stencil – maybe the head of a flower – and use it to create a matching tag.

Cheeky Chums

The 'fluffy' border behind the blue and white cat was made using mulberry paper, a fine paper with silky fibres that is actually made from the mulberry tree. I placed the stencil on the mulberry paper and 'drew' round it with a brush dipped in water leaving a 1cm (³/₈in) border. Then I gently tore the paper outwards while it was still wet. This cat was made using a single layer of card. If you want to make it stand up, cut a strip of stiff card and attach to the back of the card to use as a prop.

Hot Metal

Embossing on metal produces really dramatic effects, and is not as difficult as it looks. You do not need a light box, but you do need an unusual piece of equipment: a computer mouse mat! The reason for this is that, if you emboss metal on a flat surface, it will fold in sharp lines. If you work on the reverse of a mouse mat the yielding sponge surface results in lines that are gently curved.

For embossing on metal you will need wooden embossing tools, which are larger than metal tools. Do not try to use metal tools as they will scratch the metal foil. You will also need a wooden cocktail stick to mark out a faint line on the metal, which you then follow to emboss the lines. After embossing, the back of the raised area is filled with PVA adhesive to stop it denting.

The card is finished by mounting on several layers of card, each cut slightly smaller than the piece below. I do this by eye, so the card sizes given should be regarded as approximate.

The embossing powders

The stencils

You will need

Stencils: Dreamweaver Ginger Jar (LG626) and Celtic Heart (LL326)

Copper foil 13 x 10.5cm (5¼ x 4in)

Bronze card 21 x 13cm (8¼ x 5¼in) for mount

Green card 13 x 10.5cm (5¼ x 4in)

Gold card 13 x 10.5cm (5¼ x 4in)

Red card 13 x 10.5cm (5¼ x 4in)

Low-tack adhesive tape

Computer mouse mat

Cocktail stick

Wooden embossing tool

Wooden clothes peg

PVA adhesive

Embossing ink pad

Embossing powder: light, medium and dark metallic

Heat gun

Old scissors

Craft knife and cutting mat

Beads and a short length of wire to decorate jar

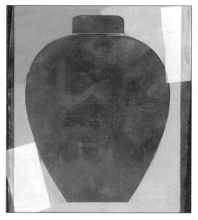

1. Working on the reverse of the mouse mat, place the jar stencil on the metal sheet. Secure with low-tack tape.

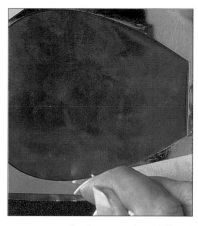

2. Using the point of a cocktail stick held at right angles to your work, trace round the outline of the jar.

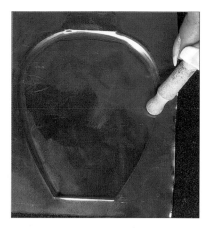

3. Turn the metal sheet over and, still working on the mouse mat, go over the outline again using the wooden tool.

4. Turn the metal sheet over. Position the heart stencil on top and fix with tape.

5. Using a cocktail stick, work carefully round the outlines of the heart design.

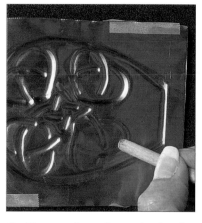

6. Turn and work on the back. Push the foil through the stencil with the blunt end of the tool.

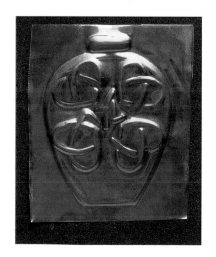

7. Turn the sheet over and remove both stencils from the front, which now has both designs raised.

8. Pat gently with the embossing ink pad to deposit small blobs of the ink randomly over the surface of the embossed design.

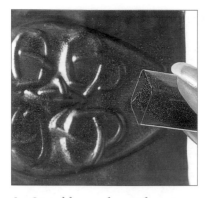

9. Sprinkle on the embossing powder, beginning with the darkest shade, to create an attractive random effect.

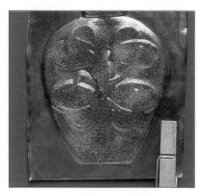

10. Sprinkle on the light and medium powders in the same random way, shaking off the excess between each stage.

11. Hold the sheet in front of the heat gun with the peg 'handle'. Heat the reverse until the powders melt and go shiny.

12. Leave to cool.

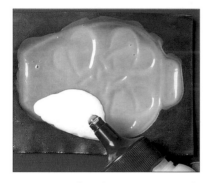

13. Turn the design over and fill the void with PVA. The photograph shows some of the PVA dry and some wet.

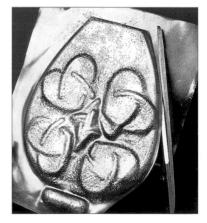

14. Leave until dry (at least two hours), then cut out the design using old scissors.

15. Thread beads on to the wire and twist it to decorate the neck of the jar. Trim the cards for the mount, starting with the red card, which should measure about 3mm (1/8in) less all round than the bronze card. Trim about 6mm (1/4in) from the gold card and 9mm (3/8in) from the green card. When you are happy with the effect, fix the layers in place with double-sided adhesive tape.

The finished card

*The embossed metal jar has been laid first on green card, then
gold, then red before mounting on bronze. There are so many
possible combinations of metal sheet and embossing powders
that this card looks different every time you make it.*

These examples were completed using the same stencils, but on card for a completely different effect. Methods of colouring include chalks (this page), chalks on metallic pearlised card (opposite, top), and pigment inks (opposite, below).

Icing on the Cake

This project uses vellum, which is also known as parchment paper. It is translucent, so it produces delicate effects that are ideal for cards for special occasions. Embossing stretches the fibres of the vellum and produces an attractive white outline. It must be done on a yielding surface, and I find the spongy reverse of a mouse mat ideal.

Vellum is easy to cut and fold, so this is an ideal project for anyone with arthritis or other problems with their hands. If, after embossing, you find you have not pressed hard enough to produce strong white lines in the vellum, try this simple solution: turn your work over and use a white crayon to strengthen them.

If you do not want to use adhesive on the vellum, punch the holes (see step 9) through the vellum and the lilac card and leave the vellum layer loose.

Vellum can be coloured in lots of different ways and the chart below shows the effect of various mediums. Your choice will depend on the effect you want: I used chalk for the card shown.

The stencil I used

You will need

Stencil: Lasting Impressions L516

Vellum 14 x 10cm (5½ x 4in)

White card 14 x 10cm (5½ x 4in)

Lilac card 12 x 8cm (4¾ x 3⅛in)

Silver card 13 x 9cm (5⅛ x 3½in)

Low-tack adhesive tape

Wax paper sheet

Chalks: green and purple

Chalk eraser and sponge applicators

Tacky craft adhesive

'Glitter glue'

Spray adhesive

Scissors

Computer mouse mat

Embossing tool with large and small ball tips

Hole punch and corner rounder

Craft knife and cutting mat

Ribbon for decoration

	Back		Front	
Chalk				
Felt-tipped pen				
Oil pastel				
Pencils				
Pigment ink				

Note

Before you work on vellum for
the first time, practise embossing
on a spare piece. Do not forget to
use a mouse mat.

1. Tape the stencil to the
reverse of the piece of vellum.

2. Rub the back of the vellum
with a piece of wax paper.

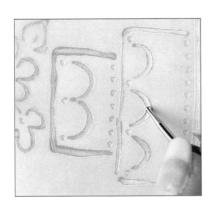

3. Place the vellum on the
mouse mat and work over
the border and design with
the large ball end of the
embossing tool.

4. Emboss the dots, holding
the tool upright and pushing
and wiggling.

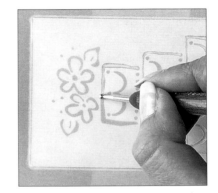

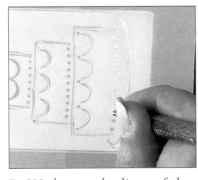

5. Work over the lines of the
design again to deepen the
lines, using the small ball tip
of the embossing tool.
Remove the stencil.

6. Cut out the embossed
design up to the line using
sharp scissors.

7. Working on the back
using a sponge applicator,
chalk in the leaves.

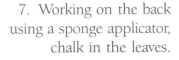

8. Add purple chalk to the flowers and swags.

9. Punch holes in the vellum above the flowers.

10. Thread ribbon through the holes in the vellum.

11. Use the corner rounder to shape all the pieces.

12. Layer the cards to check the sizes. Tie the bow.

13. Apply tacky craft adhesive to the outside edge of the reverse of the vellum to attach it to the lilac card.

14. Apply glitter glue to the flowers, swags and dots.

15. Assemble the cards and fix in place with spray adhesive or double-sided tape.

The finished card

These examples show alternative ways of attaching the vellum. This not only prevents the glue showing through the vellum, but looks attractive and a bit different. From top left, working clockwise, the vellum on the card with coloured green squares was fixed in place using eyelets. The card in shades of mauve was stitched using a large needle and fancy string. The cake card was assembled using spray adhesive and trimmed with strips of peel-off craft sticker. The design on the blue and green card was cut out using fancy craft scissors and fastened in place using bradlets.

Tiny Toes

This versatile card would be perfect as a birthday card for a little girl, or to welcome a new arrival. The variations on page 40-41 show a version made with a different stencil which is more suitable to give to a little boy.

To make the frame for the card, emboss round the straight edges of the stencil first, then emboss the details of the shoes. Take care to leave enough space between the stencil and the edge of the card before embossing. When you cut out the shoe shapes you need to leave a good margin or you will lose the embossed effect.

The card is assembled using pieces of foam tape, which hold them slightly apart and produce a 3D effect. There is a lot of detail and it may look fiddly, but you will find tweezers very helpful during the assembly process. You do not have to use as many layers of card as I have done, but I think it makes the finished card look extra-special. Complete the effect with an envelope decorated to match and trimmed with tiny rosebuds (see pages 38–39).

You will need

Shoe stencil: Lasting Impressions L9130

White card for mount 21 x 13cm (8¼ x 5¼in)

Pale green card 13 x 10cm (5¼ x 4in)

Dotted pink card 12 x 9cm (4¾ x 3½ in)

Deep pink card: will be trimmed to 10.5 x 7.5cm (4¼ x 3in)

Scraps of card in pale and deep pink, pink dotted and green

Light box

Low-tack adhesive tape

Wax paper sheet

Embossing tool with large ball tip

Fancy craft scissors

Straight scissors

Craft knife and cutting mat

Tacky craft adhesive

Tweezers

Hole punch

Double-sided adhesive tape and foam pads

The stencil

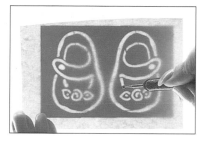

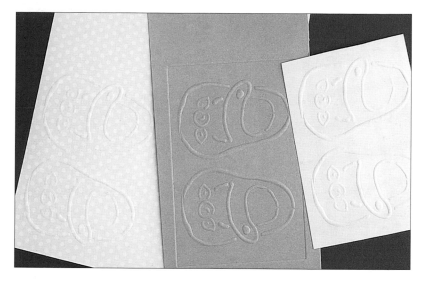

1. Fix the stencil to the deep pink card with low-tack tape and place on the light box. Wax the card and emboss shoe shapes and a frame. Emboss shoe shapes on the pink dotted and pale pink card.

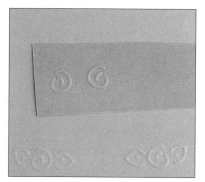

2. Emboss two roses on a scrap of deep pink card, and roses and leaves on a scrap of pale green card.

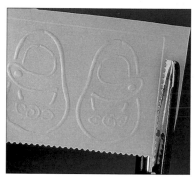

3. Cut outside the embossed frame of the deep pink card using fancy craft scissors.

4. Cut out the pink dotted shoe shapes carefully on the *inside* of the embossed line.

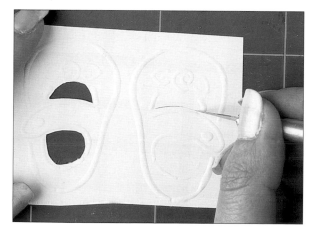

5. Place the pale pink card on a cutting mat and use a craft knife or scalpel to cut out the sections of shoe above and below the embossed straps.

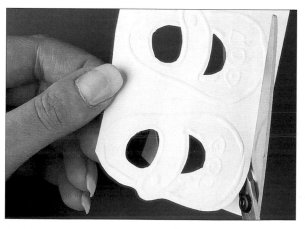

6. Using scissors, cut carefully round the shoe shapes on the outside of the line, leaving a border of at least 1mm ($^1/_{16}$in) round the embossed line.

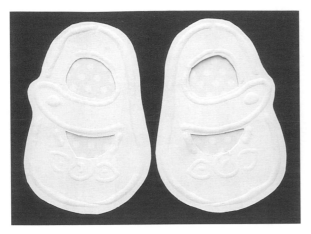

7. Place the pale pink shoe 'uppers' on the dotted 'insoles' and fix them together using tacky craft adhesive.

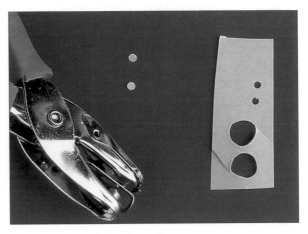

8. Using a craft knife and cutting mat, cut out the two pink rosebuds. Using a hole punch, make two tiny circles from the same card.

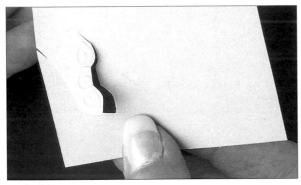

9. Using scissors, cut round the leaves and across between them to form a 'bridge' on which to place the pink rosebud.

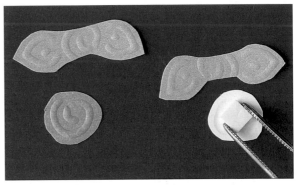

10. Using tweezers, place tiny double-sided adhesive foam pads on the back of each rosebud, then fix to the leaves.

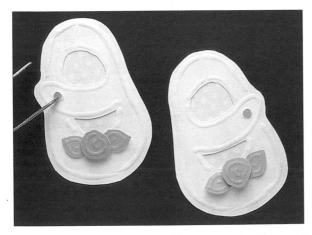

11. Place the rosebuds and leaves on the front of the shoes and the 'buttons' on the straps. Fix in place with tacky craft adhesive.

Note

To place the buttons, apply adhesive to the strap first. Moisten the end of the tweezers as it will help to pick up the dots more easily.

Make a matching envelope by gluing an embossed panel of card to the front of a plain envelope. Decorate with tiny buds and leaves.

The finished card and matching envelope

The card was completed by layering the backing cards and
fixing the shoes in place using double-sided tape.

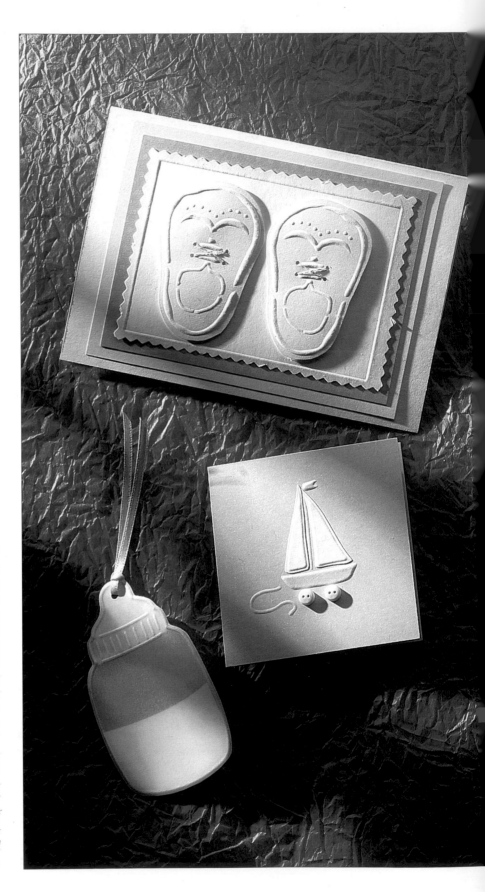

Variations

These cards were made using a variety of stencils on a nursery theme. The card featuring shoes for a boy was finished with silver thread laces. The baby's bottle gift tag (below left) was cut from vellum and outlined, then a piece of white card was placed behind the vellum to produce a convincing 'milk' effect. The top was added using embossed pastel card with a ribbon trim. The little yacht (centre left) was finished with two tiny button 'wheels' and an embossed string, and the buttons on the tiny sleepsuit (top right) were made using a hole punch. The clothes and toy on the line of 'washing' (below right) were made using scraps of card in different pastel colours, and the 'pegs' and washing line were coloured using chalk.

Festive Fun

This card introduces the blind embossing technique, which you will need if you want to work on dark colours. You cannot use a light box with dark colours as the light does not shine through the card. Instead, you follow the outlines of the stencil that are revealed when you rub wax paper on the back of the card. It leaves an impression a bit like brass rubbing, and means that you can even work on black card.

I have decorated the card with balls of glitter that stand out from the surface. The technique for this is a bit fiddly but the effect makes the effort worthwhile. To make the glitter balls, blobs of adhesive are squeezed over the design, then carefully covered with glitter so that the adhesive is not flattened. The adhesive dries and leaves a pattern of shiny 'balls' that stand out in relief. Do this in two halves: if you try to do it all at once the adhesive will form a skin and the glitter will not stick to the last few blobs.

The stencil

You will need
Stencil: Dreamweaver LG651

White card 27 x 11cm (10½ x 4¼ in) for mount

Red card 12.5 x 10cm (5 x 4in)

Green card 12 x 9.5cm (4¾ x 3¾in)

Removable adhesive tape

Embossing tool with large ball tip

Red, white and gold glitter

Teaspoon

Ruler or bone folder

Wax paper sheet

Scissors

'Dries white' glitter adhesive

Craft knife or scalpel and cutting mat

The glitters

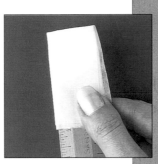
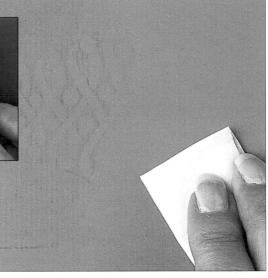

1. Attach the stencil to the green card using removable adhesive tape.

2. Fold wax paper neatly over the end of a ruler or bone folder and rub it firmly over the reverse of the card.

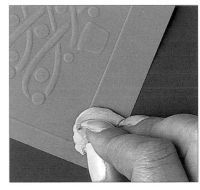

3. Outline the frame with the embossing tool, then emboss the design. Press firmly and follow the wax impression.

4. Continue until the whole design has been embossed. Remove the stencil.

5. Go over the design with adhesive putty to remove any tape residue.

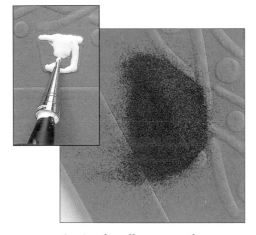
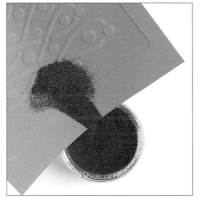

6. Apply adhesive to the pot outline, then use a spoon to cover the adhesive completely with red glitter.

7. Curve the card and use it as a funnel to replace the excess glitter in the pot.

8. Complete a gold star using glitter and adhesive.

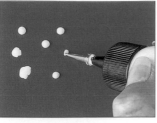

Note
Practise squeezing blobs of
adhesive on a spare piece of card
before going on to the next stage.

9. Squeeze blobs of adhesive
all over the lower section of the
embossed tree.

10. Using a spoon, sprinkle
glitter carefully round each of
the adhesive blobs.

11. Carefully sprinkle glitter
over the tops of the adhesive
blobs, then pick up the card...

12. ...and flip it to shake off
excess glitter.

13. Turn the card the right
way up and leave it to dry.
Now complete the top half.

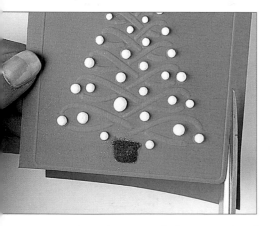

14. Cut round the outside of
the embossed frame, leaving
about 3mm ($\frac{1}{8}$in)...

15. ...and assemble the card
as shown.

The finished card

*For a completely different effect, use
several colours of glitter for the 'baubles'.*

You can really go to town when you decorate these cards. The cheeky snow people (far right) were made from the same stencil, but leaving off the heart and moving the bow from the top of the head to the neck turns the snowgirl into a snowboy! The card with the snowman holding a present (below left) was fixed to a background of torn paper strips using foam tape for a 3D effect. The glittery bauble (top left) was layered on mulberry paper and decorated with twinkly ribbon and glitter. The holly leaf (top centre) was simply decorated with glitter on 'dries-white' adhesive, and the parcels (below centre) were given extra impact with metallic card and embossed dots.

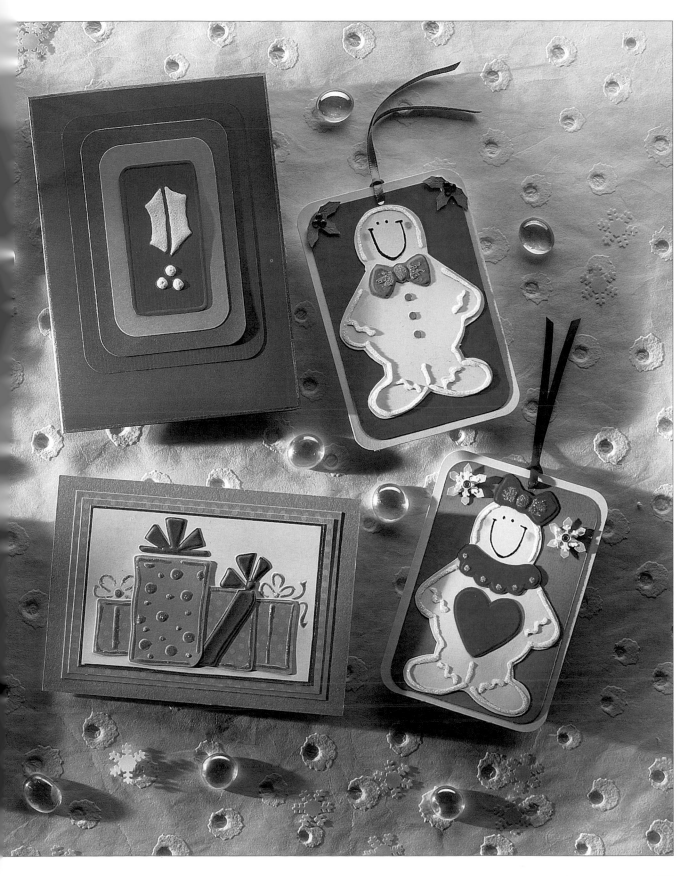

Index